Growing Responsible Kids

By Evelyn Petersen

Illustrated by Barb Tourtillotte

Totline® Publications
A Division of Frank Schaffer Publications, Inc.
Torrance, California

Dedicated with love to my children—Heather, Eric, Karin, and Kristin—and
to their children and grandchildren. I hope that you and other readers of this book
will always make it a priority to take time to enjoy activities with your children.
It is through these experiences that we cherish and honor our childhood memories.
It is during these moments that we pass on both our old and new family traditions.
Keep making moments that will last for lifetimes.   —E.P.

Managing Editor: Kathleen Cubley
Editors: Carol Gnojewski & Elizabeth McKinnon
Contributing Editors: Gayle Bittinger, Susan Hodges,
        Jean Warren
Copyeditor: Kris Fulsaas
Proofreader: Miriam Bulmer
Editorial Assistant: Durby Peterson
Graphic Designer (Interior): Sarah Ness
Layout Artist: Gordon Frazier
Graphic Designer (Cover): Brenda Mann Harrison
Production Manager: Melody Olney

ISBN: 1-57029-102-0

Library of Congress Catalog Card Number 96-61890
Printed in the United States of America
Published by Totline® Publications
Editorial Office: P.O. Box 2250
                Everett, WA 98203
Business Office: 23740 Hawthorne Blvd.
                Torrance, CA 90505

20 19 18 17 16 15 14 13 12 11 10 9 8 7 6 5 4 3 2 1

Introduction

Parents and family have the greatest impact on young children's attitudes, values, and behavior. As a parent, you are your child's best teacher, and the responsibility of modeling responsible behavior is yours. Nurturing a sense of responsibility now, when your child is young, can make a lasting difference in his or her life.

Although responsibility means different things to different people, a true sense of responsibility means that we are motivated from the inside to follow rules that help us and help others. Help your child become aware that there are many rules that both adults and children must follow to maintain healthy relationships with their family, their community, and their world.

Because children learn by doing, the way to teach them responsibility is to give them daily opportunities to be responsible. *Growing Responsible Kids* is filled with activities that are designed to help you nurture your child's inner sense of responsibility, one that is motivated not so much by obedience, but by your child's own desire to be responsible. Use the ideas in this book to teach your child about responsible behavior every day, in many simple, age-appropriate ways that are a part of ordinary family life.

A WORD ABOUT SAFETY: The activities in *Growing Responsible Kids* are appropriate for young children between the ages of 3 and 5. However, keep in mind that if a project calls for using small objects, an adult should supervise at all times to make sure that children do not put the objects in their mouth. It is recommended that you use art materials that are specifically labeled as safe for children unless the materials are to be used only by an adult.

Contents

Cultivating Self-Discipline

Making Rules and Setting Limits

Being self-aware enough to know what you can and cannot do is a sign of self-discipline. One of the best ways to begin to help your child understand what behaviors are permissible in your home is to make a few simple rules that address these limitations.

When you make rules, word them so that they reflect the behaviors that you want to encourage in your child. For example, if you want your child to stop making sculptures on your kitchen floor, you might make the following rule: "We play with modeling dough only on this table." Another rule might be "Talk very softly when baby is sleeping" or "All preschoolers in our home must take a nap after lunch." Let your child help you make family rules, and discuss why the rules are important and how they help us. When you remind your child about a rule, ask him to think and remember what the rule is about.

Children feel secure when they know what is expected of them.

Making Choices

Give your child the chance to practice decision making every day.

If you want your child to learn about self-discipline and responsibility, it's very important to give her the experience of making choices. Structure these choices so that they are appropriate for the age of your child. For example, as the parent, you must decide which breakfast cereals are healthy for your child. But you could keep a few different brands of healthy cereal on hand and let your child choose each day which one she wants. Your child can also make choices about which bedtime story to read, which toys to clean up first, or which of several outfits to wear. The older your child gets, the more choices you can make available to her.

However, don't offer your child a choice if there really is no choice. For example, if you want her to pick up her toys and get ready for bed, don't ask, "Would you like to stop playing now? Isn't it time for bed soon?" Instead, say, "In about five minutes you will need to pick up your toys and start getting ready for bed." When five minutes are up, tell her, "Now it's time to pick up. Are you going to pick up the blocks first or the cars first?"

Calming Down and Taking Breaks

Young children need to be taught how to calm themselves down periodically during their day. If your child seems unusually loud or rowdy, it may be a sign that he is overexcited or overtired. Try to become aware of these signs in your child and teach him to recognize for himself when he is losing control, becoming too loud, or moving too fast. Set clear rules or expectations for your child's play, and encourage him to take breaks often. Help him learn to pace himself by developing a special signal for break time, or by stepping in occasionally to ask if he thinks he could use a break to catch his breath and play more cooperatively. Below are some good break-time strategies.

To stay balanced and emotionally fit, everyone needs a natural rhythm in their daily activities.

- Talking quietly together
- Napping
- Snacking
- Looking at books
- Drawing
- Slow-motion activities such as pantomiming and moon walking
- Deep breathing
- Gentle exercising (bending and stretching)

When he can stop on his own and take a "calm down" break, he is truly accepting responsibility for his well-being.

Time-Out

A time-out is a disciplinary method that can be used to teach self-control. Giving your child a time-out means removing her from the scene of misbehavior. When you give your child a time-out, try to avoid shaming her or becoming emotional. Set up a chair for her to sit in quietly in a place without distractions such as a corner or hallway, and don't let her leave the chair until the time-out is over. Try to keep the duration of the time-out short and consistent; two to three minutes is all that is necessary for young children. Placing an hourglass or an alarm clock near your child during her time-out, so that she can keep track of the time, may make the discipline more bearable.

Time-outs are most effective if your child understands and can tell you what she did that was inappropriate. Explain that she needs to take time to think about a different and better way to behave. Encourage her to use the time to calm down, regain self-control, and decide she is ready to follow the rules.

When the time-out is over, there is no need to express anger or to dwell on her misbehavior. Ask her if she is ready to behave now. Then hug her and give her a chance to start over.

Encourage your child to visualize positive behavior.

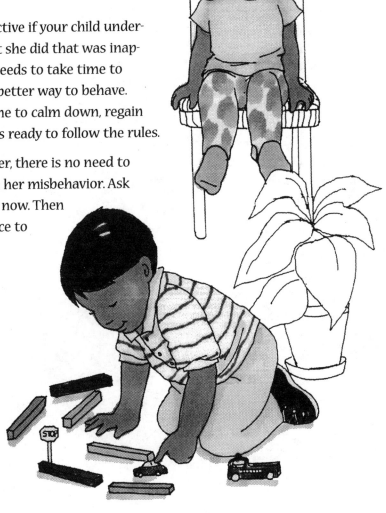

Getting Dressed

Make the process of dressing and undressing easy for your child by selecting pullover sweaters and jackets, sweatpants and sweatshirts without drawstrings, elastic-waist pants, and slip-on shoes or shoes with Velcro closures. Involve your child in choosing what to wear each day, dressing himself, and taking care of the clothes he takes off. Here are some other ways to help your child become more responsible for his clothing.

Your child will feel grown up if he has some control over what he wears.

- Let your child help you fold his clothes and put them away in his dresser or clothes closet.

- Give your child a hamper, a basket, a tote bag, or an old pillowcase with his name written on it to put his daily dirty clothes in.

- Hang clothes hangers and hooks in your child's room so that they are easy for him to reach.

- Make a shoe storage area out of crates or shoeboxes.

- Make a space near your front door for your child to hang up his outdoor clothes.

- Practice using buttons, zippers, and snaps by draping adult-size jackets or sweaters over the back of a chair.

Mealtimes

Preschoolers know how to feed themselves, so they can now take on additional responsibilities at meals. Instead of filling your child's plate, let her serve herself.

If you serve meals buffet style, make it easy for her by setting the food out on low tables. Cut portions of each food into small pieces that are easier for her to put on her plate, and include teaspoons along with larger serving spoons. Fill a plastic measuring cup with water, milk, or juice, and let your child use it as a pitcher so she can pour her own drink. Slice butter into pats, or set out tubs of soft butter or margarine so your child can butter her own roll or bread, and put condiments in squeeze containers or in small bowls so she can choose her own independently.

If you pass the food around the table "family style," use small, lightweight serving bowls and refill them often. Seat your child near the end of the passing line so the portions aren't too heavy for her to lift. If the meat is difficult to cut or if she hasn't mastered this skill yet, cut it for her ahead of time and place it on the platter. Say "please" and "thank you" when you are passing food around and set simple family guidelines about clearing the table so that everyone, including your child, is involved.

Family-style meals offer opportunities for good manners and conversation.

Bedtimes

Always prepare children ahead of time for the end of their day.

Your preschooler needs between 8 and 11 hours of sleep each night, with consistent bedtime routines and regular bedtime hours. If you set up a simple routine for him to follow, your child is old enough to get ready for bed by himself. His bedtime routine should be a calm, relaxed time of about 30 minutes. It might include a shared time when you eat a snack together, talk quietly, read a bedtime story, and tuck him in for the night. It might also include time for toileting, putting dirty clothes away, washing face and hands, and brushing teeth. Coach your child to learn this routine with your cues. "It will be time to put your pajamas on in ten minutes." Later, "Now it's time to brush your teeth." When children practice a consistent nightly routine, they feel secure and more relaxed. They also learn the discipline they'll need to get ready for bed independently.

Waking Up

Your child may be an "early bird," or she may be a late sleeper. Help her learn to be responsible about wake-up time by making sure that she goes to bed early enough each night to get a good night's sleep. If she has trouble waking up in the morning, give her a small alarm clock and help her set it every night before she goes to bed. Show her how to shut it off by herself when the alarm rings. If your child wakes up long before anyone else in your house, plan specific things for her to do by herself in her room while waiting for you to wake up. The following are a few suggestions.

Every child operates on her own internal clock.

- Select picture books the night before for her to "read" in the morning.

- Set out paper and crayons for her to use to draw a good-morning picture.

- Start a block house at bedtime and have her finish it when she wakes up.

- Rotate her toys by always keeping a few of them in storage. Then set out a different one each night for her to discover in the morning.

Nurturing a Work Ethic

Mommy's and Daddy's Jobs

Children soon learn that their parents' jobs are connected to money, and that money is exchanged to get items that the family needs or wants. Working outside the home is often necessary and is one of the most important things that parents do to cooperate as part of the family team.

To help your child begin to understand your job, arrange to take him to your workplace for a visit. Let him see where you work, observe what you do there, and meet other people you work with. Your child will learn that in your job you cooperate with other people every day. He will see that everyone works together to get things done.

If your child cannot visit your workplace, take photos to show him and talk about later. Knowing more about your job may also ease his anxiety when you are away at work and help him to be more cooperative when you are gone.

If you are a stay-at-home dad or mom, make your child aware that everything you do around the house, from washing clothes to cooking meals, is part of your job.

Being part of the family team means that parents often must work outside the home.

The Help-Out Habit

Encouraging your child to help out in small ways as a family member and to take pride in these responsibilities is the first step toward nurturing a positive work ethic. Provide your child with many opportunities for helping out around your house. If you show your appreciation for her contributions, your child will enjoy working with you, whether you ask her to fetch or carry, set the table, sort clean laundry, or scrub vegetables. Keep in mind that it is the *habit* of cooperating in this way that is important, not how perfectly she does her tasks.

Give your child many opportunities to establish the habit of helping.

The following are more ideas for jobs your preschooler can help you with.

- ✽ Taking care of pets
- ✽ Watering plants
- ✽ Washing the car
- ✽ Vacuuming the carpet
- ✽ Putting groceries away
- ✽ Dusting furniture
- ✽ Pulling weeds or bagging leaves
- ✽ Making lunch

The Allowance Debate

The topic of allowance raises a lot of questions. Should children be given an allowance? Is an allowance a right, or a privilege to be earned? At what age should children begin to receive an allowance?

Whether you decide to give your child an allowance is an individual family decision. When to begin giving your child an allowance is also up to you. If you think your child is old enough to have money, and if you are willing to help him take responsibility for the money that you give him, then you are ready to begin.

If you do decide to give him an allowance, think of it as a tool for teaching him about the value of money. Along with the money, introduce him to the concepts of spending, saving, and earning. Make behavior a separate issue from his allowance so that he won't link money with punishment or reward. If you decide to not give an allowance, consider giving your child money for small purchases when you go shopping. Or keep a change jar on hand for him to dip into with permission, so that he will have experiences in spending money.

If handled effectively, a regular allowance can be a great teaching tool.

Learning About Money

If you decide to give your child an allowance, take steps beforehand to prepare her for this privilege and responsibility. Help her understand the concept of money in terms of number and quantity by giving her the opportunity to use money in and out of your home.

At home, let your child sort and count real coins, and play pretend store with real coins. When you shop, let her help you buy items at the grocery such as cereal or fruit. Money games for children can be found in the books *A Penny Saved* and *Money Doesn't Grow on Trees* by Neale S. Godfrey.

Help your child realize that money is a medium of exchange.

Delayed Gratification

One of the hardest life lessons that your child needs to learn is that he cannot always have what he wants when he wants it. Don't rush out to buy your child the latest toy he asks for. Instead, consider teaching him about delayed gratification. Tell him that some things have to be earned, and it takes time to save up money to buy something special that you want. Give your child two containers or jars, one for money he can spend at any time, and one for money to be saved for buying something special or expensive. Encourage him to put at least a part of his money in the savings jar every week.

Help him set realistic goals about saving. If your child wants to buy a gerbil, for example, first talk with him about all of the other purchases he will need to make to keep the gerbil in your home. In two weeks, your child will probably not have saved enough money to buy a gerbil, but he may have enough to purchase gerbil food, or a wheel for it to exercise on. He may need to keep saving in order to get a gerbil cage, but he could purchase a gerbil water bottle in the meantime.

Teach your child the value of saving money to buy something special.

Learning from Choices

One way to build a foundation for responsible money management is to let your child make her own spending choices with her disposable income. Try not to interfere as she spends her money, so that she has the opportunity to learn from her spending choices.

Perhaps your child will buy candy that looks good but doesn't taste good to her. If this happens, don't replace the money. Your child needs to accept the responsibility of poor choices and learn from these experiences. If you let your child make small mistakes with a little bit of money, chances are she won't repeat the same mistakes on a larger scale.

Encourage your child to learn from her purchases.

Family Savings Bank

With your family, decide on a special event you would like to attend or a short trip that you would like to take together. Then choose a piggy bank or an unusual container in which to save money for the outing. If you like, turn an empty plastic jug into a "piggy bank" by using permanent markers, glue, and scraps of felt to make eyes, ears, a nose, and other features. Then add a curled pipe-cleaner tail and a cut-out slit for depositing money.

Decide as a family how your pig will be "fed." For instance, you might all agree to feed it a certain amount from allowances or to empty loose change into it once a week. Or, you may decide that you will put any "found" money into it. Find ways for every child in the family to "earn" money to put in the bank. When it's time to take out the money, count it together and celebrate the family's teamwork.

Your child will learn that a goal is easier to achieve when everyone contributes.

Grocery Shopping

When you are planning your grocery shopping, let your child help you in various ways. For instance, have her help count how many cans of soup you already have or look in the vegetable bin to see if you have potatoes and carrots on hand. Before going to the store, have her observe as you write out your grocery list and let her help sort your coupons.

Helping with grocery shopping lets your child experience cooperation.

When you arrive at the store, let your child help you find the items on your grocery list, encouraging her to match the pictures on the coupons to items on the shelves. Also, let her help you weigh fruits and vegetables on the produce scale. As you walk through the store, point out the different kinds of jobs store employees are doing, such as stocking shelves, taking money, and bagging groceries. These people all work as a cooperative team, just as family members work as a team to help each other.

Nurturing Family Responsibility

Belonging Is Crucial

It's important to help your child feel connected to others.

Children are often uprooted from the ties they form with friends and communities because of divorce, separation, job relocation, or unemployment. For this reason, it's all the more important to give them a strong sense of belonging to your family. Children who feel a sense of belonging are less likely to have problems getting along with others as they mature. When children feel the security of roots in their families and communities, they are better able to understand the many ways they contribute to and benefit from them.

Here are a few ways to foster feelings of belonging.

- Enlist the help of your relatives to make a family tree.
- Volunteer for a local organization and take your child to its functions.
- Write to family members on a regular basis.
- Visit family members as often as possible.
- Establish family rituals that can be carried out regardless of where you live, such as having a sing-along during the holidays or taking a walk together on the first day of spring.
- Organize a neighborhood block party.

Holding Family Meetings

Plan regular family meetings that include your child. During these meetings, take turns sharing things that you noticed and appreciated about one another's behavior as well as concerns that you feel should be aired. To emphasize cooperation and problem solving, make sure that each family member has a turn to speak and that everyone speaks calmly, politely, and candidly.

You might start your meetings by sharing positive things. Then get any complaints out into the open. Brainstorm as a team to make and/or change family rules. Use your family meetings to demonstrate honest communication, which is the basis of positive social relationships.

Use communication to develop cooperation and group problem-solving skills.

Family Manners

Using good manners is a responsible way to show respect for others. Make it a family habit to practice good manners every day. When parents get too busy or preoccupied to model good manners, young children drop this good habit very quickly.

If you notice that your child is forgetting to mind his manners, try this experiment. Set up a recorder and tape your conversation during a family meal. You may be surprised to find that you have fallen out of the habit of saying "please" and "thank you," too.

Remembering good manners is everyone's responsibility.

New Family Members

Your older child will enjoy doing many small things to help you care for your new baby. Including her in chores such as these will make her feel important and grown up.

- Fetching and carrying diapers
- Helping fold baby clothes
- Playing quietly when baby is sleeping
- Helping mix baby's rice cereal
- Helping feed baby
- Helping keep pets away from baby
- Helping sing baby to sleep
- Helping keep small toys away from baby's reach

Sibling jealousy is not usually a problem until later, when the baby can crawl and walk, and gets into big sister's things. Explain to her that all babies learn by exploring, and that the baby is too young to know that he is causing trouble. Use these incidents to teach her about cause and effect. Help her understand that when she doesn't pick up her toys, the baby will play with them. When she doesn't close her door carefully, he may try to crawl into her room.

A new baby in the house provides many opportunities to take responsibility.

The Family Team

The family is not only a group of people who live together, it is a team in which all members cooperate to help make days run smoothly for everyone. Working together makes jobs easier and faster, so there is more time for family fun.

Help your child understand that cooperative teamwork is the fair way to do things. Show him that when everyone helps out, no one person has to do an unfair share of the work. For example, if each family member cooperates by clearing his or her own place after dinner, no one person has to clear the entire table. Or, if each person puts away his or her own dirty clothes, no one person has to spend the time collecting all the dirty laundry.

Family teamwork is your young child's first experience in group cooperation.

Working With Grandparents

Supportive grandparents who live close by can usually be counted on to help out with their grandchildren, give advice, and generally be in the parents' corner through all family challenges. Whenever possible, encourage frequent visits and lots of communication between your child and your parents, and nurture common interests you see developing. If you are divorced, make sure that your child maintains a positive relationship with both sets of her grandparents.

When your ideas of parenting and the grandparents' ideas differ, try not to "sweat the small stuff." But hold firm on issues that you have strong feelings about and that involve your values. Grandparents need to understand that you are the parent, and your parental authority needs to be maintained for the emotional well-being of your child.

Don't overlook grandparents as a source of loving support for your child.

Distant Relatives

If your family is spread apart, your child may not feel connected to his extended family. He may only know or remember your distant relatives from family stories and photographs. Help strengthen these family ties by vacationing near family members, phoning regularly with your child, and arranging family reunions. Involve your child in these and other ideas for keeping in touch.

Remind your relatives that staying in touch is a mutual responsibility.

- ▧ Making short audio or video tapes
- ▧ Turning photos of your family into postcards
- ▧ Starting a family newsletter
- ▧ Sending "Thank-you" notes
- ▧ Sending greeting cards
- ▧ Beginning a story and sending it to a relative to add onto or complete
- ▧ Sending your child's paintings and drawings as gifts

Ask your distant relatives to send photos and notes to your child, and keep these items in a family scrapbook. Before visiting them, encourage them to send pictures of their house, their family, their pets, and their neighborhood to your child. These pictures will help you prepare your child for the visit and spark familiar memories when you arrive.

Honoring Family Ties

If you have gone through a divorce or a separation, be sure to maintain and encourage cooperation with all members of your child's "other" family. Invite frequent communication with her grandparents and other relatives, as well as with her noncustodial parent, if this is appropriate. Model cooperation by inviting these significant others to participate in special events that take place in your child's life, such as birthdays, holidays, or school events.

Also, encourage her to make cards and gifts to send to family members on special occasions. By doing this, you will help establish a support system and network of communication that will be available to your child whenever she needs it.

Noncustodial relatives can provide a supportive network of communication for your child.

Dealing with Family Challenges

Family Adversity

Cooperation and support are vital when families go through tough times.

Sharing the difficult times in your family's life is just as important as sharing the fun and good times. By hiding problems from their young children, parents prevent them from taking responsibility as cooperative, supportive team members.

The best way to help your child cope with a family crisis is to give him honest, accurate information, explaining the problem simply in words that he can understand. When children don't know the whole story, what they imagine can be more frightening and confusing than the truth. Truth, clearly stated, gives children more freedom to be supportive and caring.

Tattling

Tattling is a bad habit that disrupts family harmony. It can reward your child with lots of negative attention, the thrill of making you lose your temper, and the satisfaction of getting what she wants. Nip this habit in the bud by convincing your child that she will get more attention from you if she "tattles" about the positive things she sees.

The next time your child tattles, admire her observation skills. Tell her that some people such as reporters and scientists have jobs that depend on being good observers and sharing what they observe with others. Invite your child to pretend to be a reporter or scientist and observe your family. Ask her to find three good things to say about one of the members of your family.

Teach your child to put her observation skills to work for your family instead of against it.

Handling Sibling Rivalry

Young children learn a great deal about being themselves and interacting with others from the challenges of living with brothers and sisters. When they share with one another, they learn how to cooperate and compromise, even though they may do a lot of arguing in the process. If sibling rivalry is one of your family challenges, here are some tips that may reduce the arguing and stress.

There are ways to help when your children don't get along.

- Whenever possible, use humor to break the tension and then help your children use problem-solving skills to reach solutions on their own.

- Encourage teamwork in many ways, including setting family goals together and fostering open communication at family meetings.

- Give each child time alone with you so that you can observe and nurture individual strengths. Encourage each child's own interests and friendships to help your children focus on what they are able to do separately as well as together.

- Diffuse rivalry and strengthen teamwork by not taking sides. Encourage your children to take responsibility for resolving differences.

- Keep in mind that not all brothers and sisters are close when they are growing up, often because of personality differences. If this is the case in your family, accept these differences and respect them.

- Think of your home as a practice ground for life instead of a battleground for personalities.

Too Bossy?

Children who are bossy often have potentially good leadership skills, but they need to learn how to soften their approach and become more sensitive toward others. They may need to play with a broader mix of children, including older children who are less likely to tolerate being bossed, and children who exhibit bossy streaks themselves. If you have a child who tends to be bossy, here are some suggestions.

Help a child with a bossy streak improve her behavior.

- Help her develop interests through which she can meet friends.

- Encourage her potential for generosity and her ways of caring for others.

- When friends come over, remind her that they are guests and that they should be asked what kinds of play activities they prefer.

- When she is engaged in pretend play with friends, if she seems to be "directing the whole show," tactfully join in the play to involve her friends.

- If she is an only child who has difficulty with cooperation and other social skills, consider joining or forming a play group with families of other only children.

- Become involved in youth outreach or student exchange programs that will put her in touch with positive, older role models.

Helping Special-Needs Children

Overprotecting special-needs children makes it much harder for them to learn independence, life skills, and cooperation with others. All children need to learn that sometimes we cannot do things others can, but we can do our personal best. They also need to learn that sometimes friends are unkind, and that it can be hard to cooperate, especially if we think that people don't like us.

Use the same guidelines and clear expectations for a child with special needs as you would for other children. Provide consistent family routines, orderly and well-organized personal space, time for active physical play, and daily opportunities to use open-ended art materials and engage in creative activities.

Avoid making excuses or exceptions for any uncooperative or inappropriate behavior. Most important, find ways that your challenged child can help someone else who is less fortunate in some way. Ask your church leader, your doctor, your child-care director, or your volunteer center for ideas about how to accomplish this.

Children need to learn that they can cope by experiencing and resolving problems.

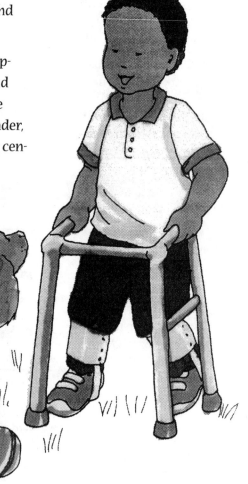

Helping Siblings of Special-Needs Children

The brothers and sisters of special-needs children have very special needs of their own. What often happens is that another child can feel left out when a special-needs child requires more attention. This feeling turns into anger and then quickly becomes guilt. The guilt often makes the child feel great pressure to overachieve. The sibling is likely to hide her feelings of stress, anger, and guilt instead of talking about them, which only makes matters worse.

Be aware that this scenario is common in families where there is a special-needs child. Make extra efforts to get siblings to be open and honest about their feelings. Thank them for their family teamwork and find ways for them to help out that they can handle without undue stress. Celebrate their achievements, but help them set realistic goals. They need lots of reassurance that they are lovable, not just capable.

If this is one of your family challenges, you may want to read Jeanne Gehret's book *I'm Somebody Too.*

Siblings of special-needs children often feel left out.

Getting Ready to Move

Moving to a new location is a common, stress-filled family challenge. Prepare your child well ahead of time, explaining that this will be an exciting project for all of you to do together. Here are some suggestions to help make the move a cooperative adventure for your child.

Moving takes full cooperation from every family member.

- Familiarize him with the process of moving, such as packing belongings, holding garage sales, and saying goodbye to your old house and neighborhood.

- Together, read library picture books about moving.

- Show him photos of the new home and its rooms. Also show photos of the new neighborhood and special community places such as the zoo or the park.

- Reassure him that he will have a place to sleep, along with his own blanket, pillow, books, and toys.

- Let him help with some of the packing.

- Remind him that he will still be able to keep in touch with old friends, but that he will make new friends too.

- Stage a moving day dress rehearsal where he can pretend to move his toys, books, and bags. After your pretend play, let him know exactly what will happen on the real moving day.

Practicing Beforehand

Children feel more secure when they can act out ahead of time a change or a new event.

You can relieve much unnecessary stress by practicing with your child before a major change or a special event. Let her role-play what will happen. For example, if you are going on a vacation and she will be flying for the first time, have her play-act what will occur at the airport. Join with her in pretending to check your baggage at the ticket counter, board the airplane, and fasten your seat belts for takeoff and landing. The following are potentially upsetting or overexciting events for young children, who may benefit from the experience of role playing.

- The birth of a new sibling
- Visiting distant relatives
- Attending a wedding
- Attending a live theatrical or musical performance
- Going to preschool or day care for the first time
- Being left alone with a babysitter overnight for the first time

Overactive Children

Most preschoolers learn through active, hands-on play. It's important to understand the stages of early childhood development so that you don't label energetic children as hyperactive or overactive when they are really just being normal.

Hyperactivity can only be diagnosed and treated by qualified and experienced professionals. Try not to let the opinions of relatives, teachers, or other parents influence you unless you have made a similar assessment of your child's behavior and activity levels. If you are really concerned about hyperactivity, ask for a free diagnostic exam through your physician or your school district's early childhood/preschool special education department. If your child does have a problem, treatment will help him learn to manage his behavior and act with more self-restraint and self-discipline.

Trust your own observations and instincts when deciding what is normal behavior for your child.

Divorce

If you are a parent who is divorced or separated and are communicating with your former spouse, it is especially important that the two of you model cooperation for your child.

At times, you may need to discuss differences privately, but make sure that you always maintain positive language, behavior, and cooperation in all matters that relate to her. She loves both of you and wants the two of you to be friends, even if you are not together.

Your child is adjusting to many changes in the family situation and needs the security that your positive interactions will provide.

Try to not make a fuss about "picky" things regarding visiting arrangements. Of course, safety is always important. But it really doesn't matter if she sleeps in a sleeping bag for a night or two or skips eating salad or vegetables for a day.

The important thing is that your child is spending special time with someone she loves.

Parents who are no longer together can still help their child learn about cooperation and caring.

Nurturing Community Responsibility

Thinking of Others

There are many ways you can help your child become more aware of the needs of others and do things that make others happy. Here are just a few of them.

- Write thank-you notes and let him add pictures and dictated messages. Send the cards to relatives and friends.

- Let him help make cookies to take to a shut-in friend.

- Show him how to use glue, felt scraps, yarn pieces, pipe cleaners, feathers, or fake fur to turn a smooth stone into a "pet rock" for a relative or a friend who cannot have a real pet.

- Have him make a get-well card or a picture to send to a friend or a relative who is ill or sick.

Your child is not too young to be caring and supportive of relatives and friends.

Community Caring and Sharing

Show your child how caring and sharing can extend to your community.

Use activities such as the ones below to help your child take part in caring for the world around her and the people in it.

⌗ Let her help when you and your neighbors work together to collect trash or clean up brush in the park.

⌗ Involve her in taking extra canned goods or outgrown clothing to a food bank or a homeless shelter.

⌗ Have her accompany you when you do volunteer work.

⌗ Take her to a senior center to drop off wildflowers or to show off her Halloween costume.

Playtime Rules

Your child will be more cooperative in playing with other children at your home if you let him help make the rules for playtime behavior.

Together, decide how many children can come to play at one time, and what should happen if there is a fight over toys or if someone hits or calls names. State your rules positively: "Modeling dough stays at the table. We share the blocks. Keep two steps apart when you climb the slide and hold on with both hands."

Before play starts, review your rules by asking, not telling. Say, "What is our rule about . . . ?" When children are asked to remember and tell, they are more likely to pay attention. Ask them to explain the reason for each rule and thank them for remembering and cooperating.

Four- and five-year-olds develop a strong sense of fairness when helping make rules.

Respecting the Property of Others

Teach your child to be as careful with the belongings of others as she is with her own.

Children understand what it means to own something. Their belongings are intensely important to them. What they need to learn is that others feel the same way about the things that they own. For example, your child may not care much about flowers, but your neighbor may prize his flower garden. When your child plays outside, she needs to respect your neighbor's feelings. If he is a close neighbor, ask him to give your family a garden tour. Let him explain how much work it takes to make his garden grow. Remind your child that the flowers in the garden belong to your neighbor, and that she must be careful not to walk on them or pick them.

When you take walks with your child, point out things in the neighborhood that people own and are proud of. Explain that it takes a long time to save up money to buy a car, rent an apartment, or build a house, and that people work hard to keep them looking nice. These explanations should help her understand why we need to respect the property of others.

Stealing

Help your child real-ize that stealing is an irresponsible behavior that hurts others. If you discover that your child has taken something, like a small toy from a toy store, the best thing to do is to remain calm. Explain to him that the toy is the property of the store, and that taking it without pay-ing for it is wrong. Tell him that if everyone took toys without paying for them, the owner wouldn't be able to buy new toys for chil-dren like him to buy.

Then take your child back to the store and make him give the toy back. Have him apologize to the owner. Be calm and polite. There is no need for blam-ing or guilt-producing lec-tures. Keep the experience a positive one so that your child won't be afraid to accept responsibility for his actions.

Responsible actions always teach more than words.

Rules in the Child-Care Center

If your child attends a preschool or a child-care center, she is familiar with group rules. Most group rules focus on personal responsibility, safety, and cooperation. Following these rules helps children practice being responsible for their own behavior outside of your home, which is a life skill you want them to learn.

If your child is having trouble following the rules, take the time to observe her as she interacts with other children in the group. As a parent and client, you have the right to ask questions. Schedule a meeting with your child's caregiver to try and discover the cause of the problem. Study the facility's group rules carefully. Think about the following as you evaluate these rules.

Keep a respectful line of communication open with your child's caregiver.

- Are the rules age-appropriate?
- Does your child clearly understand what is expected of her?
- When your child doesn't behave responsibly, what happens?
- Does your child know the reasons for each rule?
- Do the rules tell children what we want them to do instead of what we don't want? ("Sand stays in the sandbox" instead of "Don't throw sand.")

Rules in the Homes of Others

Respect and learn from rules that others follow in their homes.

Before you visit family and friends, make your child aware that rules can be different in other people's homes. Ask your family and friends to clarify their house rules. Make sure your child understands any rules that may be unfamiliar to him, and give him reminders as needed. Tell your child that along with the rules in this home, he still needs to follow your own family rules. If your friends allow their children to run in the house, but you don't allow running in your home, you can still ask your own child to "Please walk." Encourage your child to remember to say "please" and "thank you," whether or not your relatives' children do.

Rules in the Community

When you teach your child about respecting the property of others, it's also a good time to introduce the idea of public property. Explain that roads, parks, shopping centers, and sidewalks belong to all of us and are shared by many people of all ages. We need to be sure that everyone can use them easily and safely. Your child needs to know that there are rules in your community that everyone must follow, and that most of these rules are made to help keep people safe in these public areas.

Knowing community rules keeps everyone safe.

Some rules and safety skills that your child should be aware of include the following.

- Car seat and seat belt laws
- What to do at a stop sign
- What road construction signs mean
- What traffic lights mean
- How to cross streets safely
- Where to put trash in public places
- Laws regulating bikes, skates, and skateboards on sidewalks

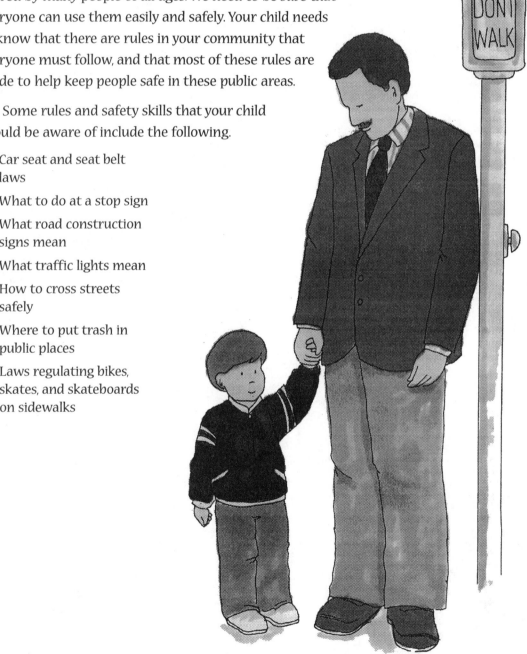

Introducing Social Skills

Being an Active Listener

Active listeners hear more than just our words. They hear what we are thinking and feeling. They listen to what is behind our words.

Practice active listening with your child. When he is speaking, try to guess what he is thinking and feeling, and ask questions that will help him say more. For instance, you might say, "It sounds like you are really angry with your friend today. Maybe your feelings are hurt. Do you want to tell me about it?" If he looks upset, you might say, "What happened to your happy smile? You look like you want to tell me something. I have time to listen." When you model active listening, your child will tell you more and will learn how he, too, can become an active listener.

Active listening is an important tool for developing social skills.

Courage and Honesty

Accepting responsibility for a mistake takes courage and honesty. These are important social skills to reinforce in your child through positive parental modeling. When you make mistakes, take responsibility for them. Try not to engage in false flattery, white lies, or half-truths in her presence. For example, avoid asking your child to say you're not at home if someone calls whom you don't want to talk to. Let your child know that telling the truth is sometimes a difficult thing to do, but it's the right thing to do.

If your child does something wrong and admits it on her own, take her honesty into consideration. Be gentle but fair about the consequences of her misbehavior, and tell her how proud you are that she had the courage to tell the truth.

The honesty and courage that your child learns in the home will affect her actions beyond the home.

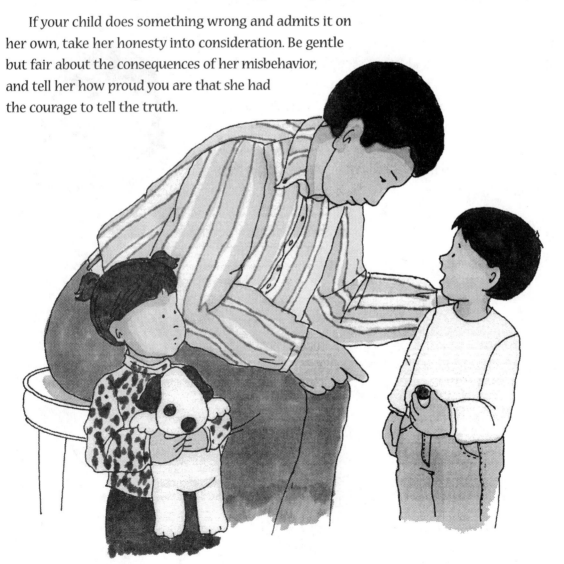

Learning About Sharing

Your child needs to learn that some toys or materials are things he shares with others. You can force him to take turns, but that's not what you really want. You want him to understand that sharing and taking turns is the right thing to do and that, if the situation were reversed, he would want others to share or take turns with him.

Children gradually learn to share and take turns, and the most important learning begins with your modeling. Let your child see you sharing and taking turns, and tell him that this is what you are doing. As a family, you share pillows on the couch, foods from serving bowls, and drinks from pitchers. You take turns with the newspaper, the toaster, the microwave, the car, the telephone, the computer, and the TV remote control. If you make your child aware of all of the sharing that occurs within your home on a daily basis, he will learn how to begin imitating this behavior.

Learning to share and take turns is a gradual process.

Sharing Feelings

Being able to share feelings leads to closer conversations with others.

Children who are able to accept and talk about both their "good" and "bad" feelings are demonstrating communication skills that will help them form solid, positive, cooperative relationships.

When they can talk freely about their feelings, fears, ideas, needs, and dreams, children become better able to listen to and empathize with others. This kind of listening and talking is the foundation for getting along well with others.

Practice these skills with your child by taking time each day to share feelings and by modeling good listening behavior for her to imitate and learn.

Positive Social Talk

Family times such as mealtimes offer parents many opportunities to model the positive language that children need to learn in order to be socially skilled. For instance, at mealtimes you may find your child imitating you when you model such phrases as "Thank you," "Please pass the butter," or "Excuse me."

If your child forgets a phrase you have taught him to use when making a request, it's easy to say, "How do we ask for the milk?" Congratulate your child on his good manners and continue to use them yourself.

Positive social language is the cornerstone of good manners.

Using Descriptive Talk

Descriptive talk is the kind of communication that improves social skills.

Descriptive comments tell others what we really mean or what we really like or dislike. When speaking with your child, use descriptive comments, encouragement, and explanations. Describe what you see her doing and what you feel and think about it. Below are a few examples of how you might do this.

- "You're using a lot of green in that painting. Green is a color that makes me feel peaceful, like when I lie on the grass and look up at the trees."

- "I see that you're making something interesting with the blocks. Can you tell me about it?"

- "I can see that you're angry with your brother. Tell him in words how you feel and what you want."

- "Thank you! It was really thoughtful of you to remember how much I like pine cones and to find one for me on your walk with Grandma."

Assertiveness

Assertiveness is the confidence and ability to tell others what we want or need without raising our voice or using hurtful remarks. Teach your child to be assertive in communicating his feelings and needs. Show him how he can do this calmly, without anger or aggression. Help him practice and refine this skill at home, stressing the use of clear communication and a quiet voice.

For instance, if he is having a problem with a classmate who engages in name-calling behavior, try this. Have him practice standing tall, pretending to look the classmate in the eye, and saying calmly and clearly, "I don't like to be called names, and I'm not going to stay here and listen to them. This hurts my feelings, so I'm leaving now."

Assertiveness can be expressed nonverbally through confident body language.

Modeling Cooperation

One of the best ways to teach your child cooperation is to make her aware of how people around her practice it. Let her see ways that you cooperate with others when friends or relatives come to visit. Point out that everyone helps by bringing different foods when there is a party or an event, and that everyone helps clean up afterward.

If you attend church, let your child see how you help out as a teacher or an usher or by taking part in potlucks, bake sales, or bazaars. When your neighbors or community members work together on an event such as a school fundraiser or block party, point out the various ways that people work together to get the job done.

Remember that your child is paying attention to what you do and say. If you want her to feel that cooperation is a positive experience, not a boring duty, make sure that you maintain a positive attitude yourself.

Your child will learn about cooperation by observing you.

Problem-Solving Steps

When safety is not a factor, always try to let children be responsible for resolving their own disagreements. Instead of jumping in to referee, be a facilitator, helping them to solve problems by following the steps below.

1. Ask each child to explain what is happening. Practice active listening to encourage the children to say more about the problem, how they feel about it, or what they wish could happen.

2. Ask the children to think of different ways to solve the problem. (Three- and four-year-olds may need to be prompted by questions.)

3. Have the children choose one of their solutions and let them try it out.

4. Help the children evaluate the solution. If it didn't work, encourage them to try an alternative solution.

Some books you might read about problem solving are Myna Shure's *Raising a Thinking Child*, Elizabeth Crary's *Kids Can Cooperate*, and the Totline *Problem Solving Safari* series by Barbara Backer and Susan Miller.

Children can learn how to resolve their own differences.

Tact and Truth

You can help your child learn how to be truthful and tactful at the same time.

Teach your child how to tell the truth without hurting someone else's feelings. If a friend gives her a gift of a book or a toy that she already has, she needs to know how to thank the gift-giver with tact as well as truth. It's a good idea to prepare your child before gifts are given with meaningful things she can say besides "Thank you." For instance, she could say, "I really like this book," or "Thanks, I'm really glad you could come to my party," or "Thanks for being my friend and giving me this present." Stress that giving a gift is a way of showing caring, and that the thought counts more than the gift.

Nurturing Anti-Bias Attitudes

Different Is Interesting

Today's children will live and work in a world that is fast becoming a global village. They will need to know how to cooperate successfully with people from different backgrounds, cultures, and religions. This is why it is so important for your child to learn positive attitudes about differences in others.

Children are not born with biases and prejudices, but they learn them quickly from what others say or do.

You can combat bias by showing your child that different does not mean better or worse—different is simply different, and quite interesting. Point out simple differences among members of your own family, your friends, and your neighbors. Try not to focus on physical differences only, but on the different ways people work, play, and think. As your child's world expands and he meets different kinds of people, expand your teaching.

Positive attitudes about differences in others is one of the most important things you can teach.

Special-Needs Children

Teach your child that sometimes special-needs children have special challenges that make it necessary for them to act or do things differently. Explain that some of these children often need special tools such wheelchairs, neck braces, eyeglasses, or hearing aids to make it easier for them to see, hear, move, or play on their own. Let her know that these tools aren't toys, and that children with special needs depend on them to stay safe.

When you have the opportunity, point out to your child people who have achieved success in spite of disabilities. Be conscious of the way that people with special needs are represented in the books, magazines, and television programs that you share with her. If she attends a school or child-care center, encourage her teachers or caregivers to borrow a wheelchair, walker, or crutches for the children to examine and use. To extend learning at home, put eyeglasses (with the lenses removed) in your child's dress-up box. Teach her about signing and regularly use simple words and phrases in sign, such as "work," "play," "hug," and "I love you."

Understanding disabilities will help your child make friends with those with special needs.

Homes

Help your child understand that people live in various kinds of homes. These dwellings may not all look the same, but they are all homes in which people live. Start by pointing out different kinds of homes in your neighborhood. Do people live in houses of different colors, shapes, sizes, and materials? Do they live in duplexes or in various kinds of apartment houses? What about in condos, mobile homes, or RVs?

Follow up by showing your child pictures of homes found in other parts of the country or the world. Compare the colors, sizes, and shapes of the homes and the materials from which they are made. Talk about fun things you could do if you lived in these homes.

There are many kinds of "houses" and all of them are homes.

oods

Whenever possible, include foods from other regions and countries in your family meals. You might want to start by introducing various kinds of breads. Everyone, all over the world, eats bread of some kind. Help your child come to understand that although the breads may be different in some ways, they are all breads that people need and like to eat.

Purchase different kinds of breads for your family, one at a time, to eat along with what you usually buy. Try pita breads, French or Italian breads, tortillas, fry bread, cornbread, rye bread, and so forth. Talk about the tastes and textures of each bread. Also, use a map or a globe to show your child the countries in which the breads originated. Continue by gradually including new kinds of fruits or vegetables in your family meals.

Tasting a variety of breads introduces your child to differences in foods.

Music

Honor diversity enjoyably through the universal language of music.

 Expose your child to different kinds of music, from rock and roll to blues, jazz, and classical. Try to purchase and listen to music that reflects a variety of cultures and lands. Compare the harmonies and rhythms. (The music of the Republic of South Africa is very different from the music of Morocco, for instance.) On some radio stations, you can listen to Latino music from many countries. On college and public radio stations you are likely to hear music from every continent and from countries all over the world.

Give your child a scarf, find one for yourself, and try waving them as you dance to different kinds of music. From Scottish bagpipe melodies to Native American flute songs, music is infinitely varied, and all of it can be enjoyable.

Broadening Horizons

With your child, look for library picture books about children of other cultures. Read about children with different backgrounds in our own country, not just in other lands. When looking for books about difference, bias, and prejudice, be sure to include Dr. Seuss's *The Sneetches and Other Stories*. These stories deal with anti-bias issues using situations that children can relate to, such as being excluded from games and parties, or being afraid of someone until meeting them and finding out what they're like. The inventive language engages young children while broadening their awareness.

Also, collect magazine pictures of children and adults from different cultures who show a variety of expressions such as surprise, fear, joy, anger, sadness, and excitement. Cut out the pictures, mount them on cardboard or posterboard, and cover them with clear self-stick paper. Use the pictures to talk with your child about feelings. Help her to understand that all people have the same kinds of feelings, no matter what their age or appearance.

Teach your child about the differences and similarities among various cultures.

Who Are Your Friends?

If you want your child to feel comfortable about making friends with a variety of kinds of people, model that behavior yourself. When you go to the park with him, make it a point to talk to other parents of different cultures who are there with their children. You can also do this on the bus, in the grocery store, at group meetings, in the doctor's office, and so forth.

By these actions your child will get the message that you do not speak to and enjoy only "certain" parents but all parents. Encourage family friendships with a diversity of people of various ages from different backgrounds and cultures.

Show your child that you enjoy diversity in friendships.

Cowboys and Indians

Try to avoid letting your child misrepresent native cultures by role-playing or reenacting events of centuries ago that she cannot understand. Play activities such as "Cowboys and Indians" reinforce competitive and negative attitudes toward Native Americans. If her child-care center plans an activity such as a Pilgrim and Indian feast at Thanksgiving, voice your objections on the grounds that the children don't understand the historical and social context surrounding these events. Suggest planning a harvest feast and inviting Native Americans to visit the center to explain their tribal nation's harvest celebrations and how they continue to honor them with traditional festivities.

Expose your child to age-old Native American skills and talents such as farming, fishing, leather work, stonework, storytelling, music, and dance. Together, visit art exhibits and museums to see the fine paintings, pottery, baskets, carvings, weavings, and jewelry from various Native American cultures.

Encourage similar exploration into the arts and customs of other native cultures.

Help stop stereotyping before it starts.

Gender Traps

Make sure you offer all kinds of activities, toys, and books to your child, regardless of gender. Check how you've done so far by making a quick and honest inventory of the kinds of toys, books, and activities you have in your home. Do you have dolls (besides action figures) for a boy to play with? Does a girl have a selection of cars and trucks? Does your child play with blocks and other construction materials regardless of gender?

In what sorts of activities do you encourage your child's participation? Is a boy encouraged to help make cookies, and is a girl given simple tools to experiment with? What kinds of children's books do you have? Make any changes or additions needed to help your child feel that boys and girls have equal potential and talents.

Let your child's potential, and not his gender, guide your activity choices.

Correcting Misconceptions

Speak out whenever you hear a hurtful or untrue comment to help your child avoid bias and prejudice.

One of the most important things you can do to combat bias and prejudice is to immediately correct any misconceptions your child expresses about other children or adults who appear different in some way. ("His nose is too big." "Her eyes are funny looking." "Girls can't drive trucks." "Boys can't play house." "Old people are no fun." "Poor people like junk and are always dirty.")

If you hear such a remark, whether it comes from your child or a friend, speak up calmly, stating that you do not approve of what was said and explaining that the remark is either hurtful or untrue. If appropriate, ask questions to find out the reason for the remark, then correct the misconception. Encourage a healthy attitude toward differences by answering your child's questions honestly and fostering pride, not superiority. When you say nothing, you are giving silent approval. This hurts your child and others. It will foster bias and prejudice and impede the fostering of cooperation.

Cultivating Evironmental Awareness

Environmental Awareness

Young children can easily learn that they are a part of the natural world and that their actions have an impact on the environment. But before they can feel any responsibility to the environment, they need to become aware that plants, animals, and people all depend on each other, and that all things in nature work together.

Talk about how every living plant or animal depends on other plants and animals to survive. People depend on animals for food and companionship, and on plants for food and clean air.

Some animals depend on people to give them food, some animals eat other animals for food, and some animals depend on plants for food and shelter. Plants are affected by the actions of people and animals.

Plants and animals die and make the soil rich for new plants to grow. Soil nourishes seeds and keeps them warm and moist enough to grow into plants.

When we teach children about nature, we are teaching them the concept of interdependence. Learning about interdependence nurtures responsibility. There are many books about the environment at your local library. One excellent resource is Edward Duensing's *Talking to Fireflies, Shrinking the Moon: A Parent's Guide to Nature Activities.*

Children need to understand their role in the environment.

Caring for a Plant

Your child can learn responsibility by growing and caring for a small plant. Let your child plant seeds that grow fast, such as radish, lettuce, or marigold seeds, in small peat pots, milk cartons, or egg cartons. When the baby plants start growing, help her transplant them to flower pots or window planters. You can also root a cutting from some house plants, such as spider plants, by putting the cutting in a glass of water on a window sill.

When the roots develop, she can pot and care for the plant. Teach her the importance of providing enough water, light, and soil for her plants to grow and stay healthy. Read books and magazines together that talk about the plants that you have in your house. Help your child designate one day of the week to water and care for her plants. Show her how to remove dead leaves and stems so the plant will nourish only its living parts, and provide her with a small watering can so she can water her plants easily. Demonstrate how to clean and refresh a plant's leaves by "misting" them with water from a spray bottle, and have your child carry a rag or a dishtowel to wipe up watering spills.

Plants are living things that respond to care and attention in many of the same ways that people do.

Gardening

Maintaining a garden can be a fun and rewarding family challenge.

If you don't have the space or sun for a small vegetable garden, try making a container garden with your child. With a little creativity, you can turn a balcony, a porch, or a windowsill into a garden space. Buckets, barrels, flower pots, window boxes, hanging planters, plastic dishpans, and plastic tubs are just a few of the many containers that you can use to grow fresh flowers, vegetables, and herbs.

Plan your garden together and let your child help choose what you grow. Try to vary your planting so that you can enjoy a long growing season. Put your child in charge of watering and weeding the plants. As the plants grow, discuss their characteristics with your child. Point out that often the flowers become the food to be harvested. When a vegetable or herb is ready to harvest, let your child help prepare it as part of a family meal.

Caring For a Pet

If your child enjoys caring for a plant, he may be ready for the responsibility of helping to care for a small animal. If you already have a pet or pets in your home, be sure to involve him in their care and feeding. Your preschooler may not be ready to water, feed, or brush your pet on his own, but he can help you wash the pet dishes, measure out the pet food, exercise your pet, or calm your pet while you brush it, groom it, or give it medicine.

If you don't already have a pet, with your child, visit a pet store or a friend who has pets and watch his behavior. If he is curious and responds lovingly and gently toward the animals, consider giving him a pet of his own. Discuss with your whole family the responsibilities of having a pet. Point out the similarities and differences between caring for a pet, caring for a plant, and caring for one another. Kittens, guinea pigs, turtles, or goldfish are good choices for "easy care" first pets.

Experiencing the affection of a pet can lead to respect for all animals.

Trees

Inexpensive packages of tree seedlings can be ordered from the National Arbor Day Foundation.

Go on a tree hunt with your child around your home to find some of the objects that are made from or use wood products. Then, take a walk in your neighborhood and look at the trees and shrubbery. With the help of books, see if you can identify the names of the trees you find.

Let your child "adopt" a mature tree that is growing nearby, grow a seedling in a large planter, or help him plant a young tree seedling in your yard. If your child has adopted a mature tree, he will enjoy visiting his tree every season to notice and document its changes. Encourage him to examine what is found under the tree, make leaf or bark rubbings, name the tree, talk to it, sing to it, sit under it to think or read, have a snack or a picnic under it, or lie under it to look at the sky. If the tree is on your property, perhaps he'll want to hang a wind chime, bird feeder, or tire swing from its branches. When you visit the tree with your child, discuss the many ways trees help us.

- They protect us from sun or wind.
- They help hold the soil so it doesn't wash away.
- They are home to many animals.
- They provide beauty in all seasons.
- They provide us with fuel for fires.
- They give us flowers, fruits, and nuts.
- They provide us with wood for making houses, toys, furniture, and paper.
- They create many kinds of jobs, including forest rangers, carvers, carpenters, printers, loggers, tree trimmers, landscapers, and toy or furniture makers.
- They "breathe" carbon dioxide and "exhale" oxygen, freshening the air.

*211 N. 12th St., Lincoln, NE 68508

Animal Watchers

Encourage your child to feel excitement and respect toward animals by helping her notice the variety of wild birds and other animals that come near your home.

Show your child that when birds eat seeds or find worms, they often take food into their beak and fly away to their nest to feed their babies. How is this like what moms and dads do? Squirrels stuff their cheeks full of food and run to their burrows. Might they be feeding their babies too?

Observing animals with your child is a great way to help her form connections with nature.

Also encourage interest in animals that live outside your neighborhood. Read your child books about wild animals and their habitats and behaviors. Visit a farm or a ranch to show her how people and animals can live and work together. Ask a beekeeper to explain that in the hive all the bees have jobs to do to help the group, just like the jobs that family members do to support the family.

Or get your child an ant farm so that she can see for herself how ants work together for the group.

Take your child on field trips to the zoo, a veterinarian, and an animal shelter to learn about the many things adults do to help animals. Sometimes the zoo or the Humane Society needs volunteers to help with special events and to raise money. Volunteers may also help vets feed and care for the animals.

When young children see parents, adults, and older children volunteer in support of animals, they often become volunteers themselves when they are older.

Composting

Obtain a gallon or a half-gallon jar and fill it with damp soil. Put a few holes in the lid of the jar, and have your child place various items between the dirt and the glass. Include a few of the following items.

- A piece of carrot
- An apple core
- A gum wrapper
- A piece of foil
- A piece of bread
- A flower
- A piece of plastic foam
- A piece of plastic

Composting takes time and hard work, but the benefits to the environment are worth the effort.

Have your child watch the items in the jar for several weeks. He will discover that some things disappear into the soil and become part of it, but others do not disappear and do not change at all. This is an excellent way to teach your child about composting.

After he has learned which things disappear and become part of the soil, your child can help you start a compost pile. Let him help you carry organic materials, such as grass cuttings, leaves, peelings, fruit cores, and vegetable scraps, to a bin or a dirt pile used for this purpose. Help him stir this "mix" with a small shovel to create a rich fertilizer.

Recycle

Explain to your child that we throw away a lot of trash, and that one way to throw less away is to use it again. Let your child help you sort through your trash to find recyclables. See if she can think of new ways to reuse some of these objects. Show her the recycling bins in or near your home and have her help you prepare your recyclables for storage by breaking down boxes and washing bottles and cans. Let her watch for the garbage or recycling truck, and see how the items are carried away.

Follow up discussions about recycling with reminders to help prevent littering.

Here are a few additional recycling ideas to practice with your child.

- Use newspaper, brown paper grocery bags, and magazines for art creations.
- Find places to take outgrown clothing and toys, so that others can use them.
- Use fabric remnants to make stuffed toys or pillows.
- Use berry baskets to store small toys.
- Take used magazines to a homeless shelter or to the school's art station.

Conserving Water

Teach your child how important it is to conserve water.

There are many things that your child can do to help conserve water. Teach him how to turn off the faucet while he brushes his teeth or soaps his hands, and to turn it back on only when he's ready to rinse. Keep a pitcher of water in the refrigerator so that he doesn't have to run the tap to get the water cold. Give him short showers instead of tub baths when needed.

Reinforce the importance of conserving water by not letting the faucet run with this experiment. Set a plastic tub inside your sink to catch the water as he washes his hands. Then give your child measuring cups to help you discover how much water he used. You may be surprised at how quickly the tub gets filled.

Pollution

Make your child aware of the many different things that can make our air and water so dirty that we cannot use it. Point out pollutants to your child when you encounter them in your daily life. When you walk in a parking lot after a rain, show your child the gasoline rainbows in the puddles. Explain that it's very hard to get the oil and gas out of the water. When you are driving, point out the smoke that blows from the exhaust pipes in the cars around you. Explain that the exhaust can pollute the air and make it unhealthy to breathe.

Let your child know that there are many ways that communities and families can control pollution. Visit your local water plant so that he can see how water is treated to make it safe to drink. The next time you need a vehicle emissions test, take your child along. Make clean air a priority in your car and home by enforcing a rule to not smoke indoors. Let your child help you choose plants for each room in your home to help purify and humidify the air.

Help your child understand that the effects of pollution can be minimized with responsible teamwork.

Title Index

Activity Books

BEST OF TOTLINE® SERIES
Totline Magazine's best ideas.
Best of Totline
Best of Totline Parent Flyers

BUSY BEES SERIES
Seasonal ideas for twos and threes.
Busy Bees—Fall
Busy Bees—Winter
Busy Bees—Spring
Busy Bees—Summer

CELEBRATION SERIES
Early learning through celebrations.
Small World Celebrations
Special Day Celebrations
Great Big Holiday Celebrations
Celebrating Likes and Differences

EXPLORING SERIES
Versatile, hands-on learning.
Exploring Sand
Exploring Water
Exploring Wood

FOUR SEASONS
Active learning through the year.
Four Seasons—Art
Four Seasons—Math
Four Seasons—Movement
Four Seasons—Science

GREAT BIG THEMES SERIES
Giant units designed around a theme.
Space • Zoo • Circus

LEARNING & CARING ABOUT
Teach children about their world.
Our World
Our Town

PIGGYBACK® SONGS
*New songs sung to the tunes
of childhood favorites!*
Piggyback Songs
More Piggyback Songs
Piggyback Songs for Infants
   and Toddlers
Holiday Piggyback Songs
Animal Piggyback Songs
Piggyback Songs for School
Piggyback Songs to Sign
Spanish Piggyback Songs
More Piggyback Songs for School

PLAY & LEARN SERIES
Learning through familiar objects.
Play & Learn with Magnets
Play & Learn with Rubber Stamps
Play & Learn with Photos
Play & Learn with Stickers
Play & Learn with
   Paper Shapes & Borders

1•2•3 SERIES
Open-ended learning.
1•2•3 Art
1•2•3 Games
1•2•3 Colors
1•2•3 Puppets
1•2•3 Reading & Writing
1•2•3 Rhymes, Stories & Songs
1•2•3 Math
1•2•3 Science
1•2•3 Shapes

THEME-A-SAURUS® SERIES
Classroom-tested, instant themes.
Theme-A-Saurus
Theme-A-Saurus II
Toddler Theme-A-Saurus
Alphabet Theme-A-Saurus
Nursery Rhyme Theme-A-Saurus
Storytime Theme-A-Saurus
Multisensory Theme-A-Saurus

Parent Books

A YEAR OF FUN SERIES
Age-specific books for parenting.
Just for Babies • Just for Ones
Just for Twos • Just for Threes
Just for Fours • Just for Fives

BEGINNING FUN WITH ART
Introduce your child to art fun.
Craft Sticks • Crayons • Felt
Glue • Paint • Paper Shapes
Modeling Dough • Tissue Paper
Scissors • Rubber Stamps
Stickers • Yarn

BEGINNING FUN WITH SCIENCE
Spark your child's interest in science.
Bugs & Butterflies • Plants &
Flowers • Magnets • Rainbows
& Colors • Sand & Shells
• Water & Bubbles

LEARNING EVERYWHERE
*Discover teaching opportunities
everywhere you go.*
Teaching House • Teaching Trips
Teaching Town

Story Time
*Delightful stories with related activity
ideas, snacks, and songs.*

KIDS CELEBRATE SERIES
Kids Celebrate the Alphabet
Kids Celebrate Numbers

HUFF AND PUFF® SERIES
Huff and Puff's Snowy Day
Huff and Puff
   on Groundhog Day
Huff and Puff's Hat Relay
Huff and Puff's April Showers
Huff and Puff's
   Hawaiian Rainbow
Huff and Puff Go to Camp
Huff and Puff's Fourth of July
Huff and Puff
   Around the World
Huff and Puff Go to School
Huff and Puff on Halloween
Huff and Puff on Thanksgiving
Huff and Puff's Foggy Christmas

NATURE SERIES
The Bear and the Mountain
Ellie the Evergreen
The Wishing Fish

Resources

BEAR HUGS® SERIES
Encourage positive attitudes.
Remembering the Rules
Staying in Line
Circle Time
Transition Times
Time Out
Saying Goodbye
Meals and Snacks
Nap Time
Cleanup
Fostering Self-Esteem
Being Afraid
Saving the Earth
Being Responsible
Getting Along
Being Healthy
Welcoming Children
Respecting Others
Accepting Change

MIX & MATCH PATTERNS
Simple patterns to save time!
Animal • Everyday
Holiday • Nature

PROBLEM SOLVING SAFARI
Teaching problem solving skills.
Problem Solving—Art
Problem Solving—Blocks
Problem Solving—Dramatic Play

Problem Solving—Manipulatives
Problem Solving—Outdoors
Problem Solving—Science

101 TIPS FOR DIRECTORS
Valuable tips for busy directors.
Staff and Parent Self-Esteem
Parent Communication
Health and Safety
Marketing Your Center
Resources for You
   and Your Center
Child Development Training

101 TIPS FOR
PRESCHOOL TEACHERS
Creating Theme
   Environments
Encouraging Creativity
Developing Motor Skills
Developing Language Skills
Teaching Basic Concepts
Spicing Up Learning Centers

101 TIPS FOR
TODDLER TEACHERS
Classroom Management
Discovery Play
Dramatic Play
Large Motor Play
Small Motor Play
Word Play

1001 SERIES
Super reference books.
1001 Teaching Props
1001 Teaching Tips
1001 Rhymes & Fingerplays

SNACKS SERIES
Nutrition combines with learning.
Super Snacks
Healthy Snacks
Teaching Snacks
Multicultural Snacks

Puzzles & Posters

PUZZLES
Kids Celebrate the Alphabet
Kids Celebrate Numbers
African Adventure
Underwater Adventure
Bear Hugs Health Puzzles
Busy Bees

POSTERS
We Work and Play Together
Bear Hugs Sing-Along
   Health Posters
Busy Bees Area Posters